a gift for:

from:

Copyright © 2017 Hallmark Licensing, LLC

Published by Hallmark Gift Books,
a division of Hallmark Cards, Inc.,
Kansas City, MO 64141
Visit us on the Web at Hallmark.com.

All rights reserved. No part of this publication
may be reproduced, transmitted, or stored in any
form or by any means without the prior written
permission of the publisher.

Editorial Director: Theresa Trinder
Editors: Kim Schworm Acosta and Keely Chace
Art Director: Chris Opheim
Designer: Scott Swanson
Production Designer: Dan Horton
Contributing Writers: Andrew Blackburn, Keely Chace,
Cheryl Hawkinson, Jake Gahr, Sarah Magill,
Amy Trowbridge-Yates, Melissa Woo, Melvina Young

ISBN: 978-1-63059-826-6
BOK1068

Made in China
0324

FIERCE LOVE

It's a **MAMA BEAR** thing.

BIG BAD WORLD, BACK OFF, BEWARE: THIS CUB'S GOT A MAMA BEAR.

A Mama Bear

STANDS UP, SPEAKS OUT,
FIGHTS HARD, FEARS NOT,
HOLDS ON, HUGS TIGHT,
AND ABOVE ALL,
LOVES LIKE YOU WOULDN'T BELIEVE.

WHERE MAMA BEARS COME FROM

Storks don't bring them.
They aren't taught or hatched or born.
Instead, she shows up
the moment she first holds
her child in her arms.

And she is amazing.

SURROUNDED BY FAMILY IS PRETTY MUCH HER NATURAL HABITAT.

HER SPIRIT ANIMAL USED
TO BE A BUNNY...
UNTIL SHE BECAME A MOM.

NOTHING SHE WOULDN'T DO FOR THE ONES SHE LOVES.

(ALSO, NOTHING ANYONE CAN DO TO STOP HER.)

SIGN #19
YOU'RE A MAMA BEAR

You make a pretty great cheering section all by yourself.

MAMA BEAR TO-DO LIST

1. Make sure everyone is taken care of.

2. Double-check.

3. Repeat.

SHE'S SMART, STRONG, AND JUST THE RIGHT AMOUNT OF SCARY.

FROM LOW-KEY TO HIGH ALERT IN

0.000001 SECONDS.

IT'S A MAMA BEAR THING.

SHE'S SMARTER, WISER, WARMER, AND WAY MORE *Wonderful* THAN YOUR AVERAGE BEAR.

SIGN #26
YOU'RE A MAMA BEAR

You do not play games . . . unless it's Candy Land or Memory, and in that case, bring it.

SHE GIVES EVERYTHING
AND STOPS AT NOTHING.

Mama Bear

JUST THE RIGHT MIX
OF CUDDLY TEDDY
AND FIERCE GRIZZLY.

SIGN #33
YOU'RE A MAMA BEAR

You have resting "I'd like to see you try" face.

UNTIL HER CHILDREN ARE STRONG ENOUGH TO STAND ON THEIR OWN, SHE IS THEIR STRENGTH.

And even after that, she goes right on being strong for them.

SHE SHOWS HOW A MOTHER'S LOVE CAN BE SOFT AS A WHISPER ONE MOMENT AND STRONG AS A HURRICANE THE NEXT.

SHE RAISES HER FAMILY DAILY.

(AND RAISES HELL AS NEEDED.)

LOVE IS POWERFUL.
SHE IS PROOF.

Mama Bear

SOMETIMES TENDER LOVE.
SOMETIMES TOUGH LOVE.
ALWAYS LOTS OF LOVE.

HOW TO WAKE A SLEEPING MAMA BEAR:

1. Be her child.

2. Be sick or alarmed or similarly in need.

3. Otherwise, do not attempt. She works hard and needs her rest!

SHE'S ALWAYS THERE. KINDA LIKE A DEVOTED STALKER WITHOUT THE BINOCULARS AND FAKE ONLINE PROFILE.

Mama Bear Motto:

I'll hibernate when I'm dead.

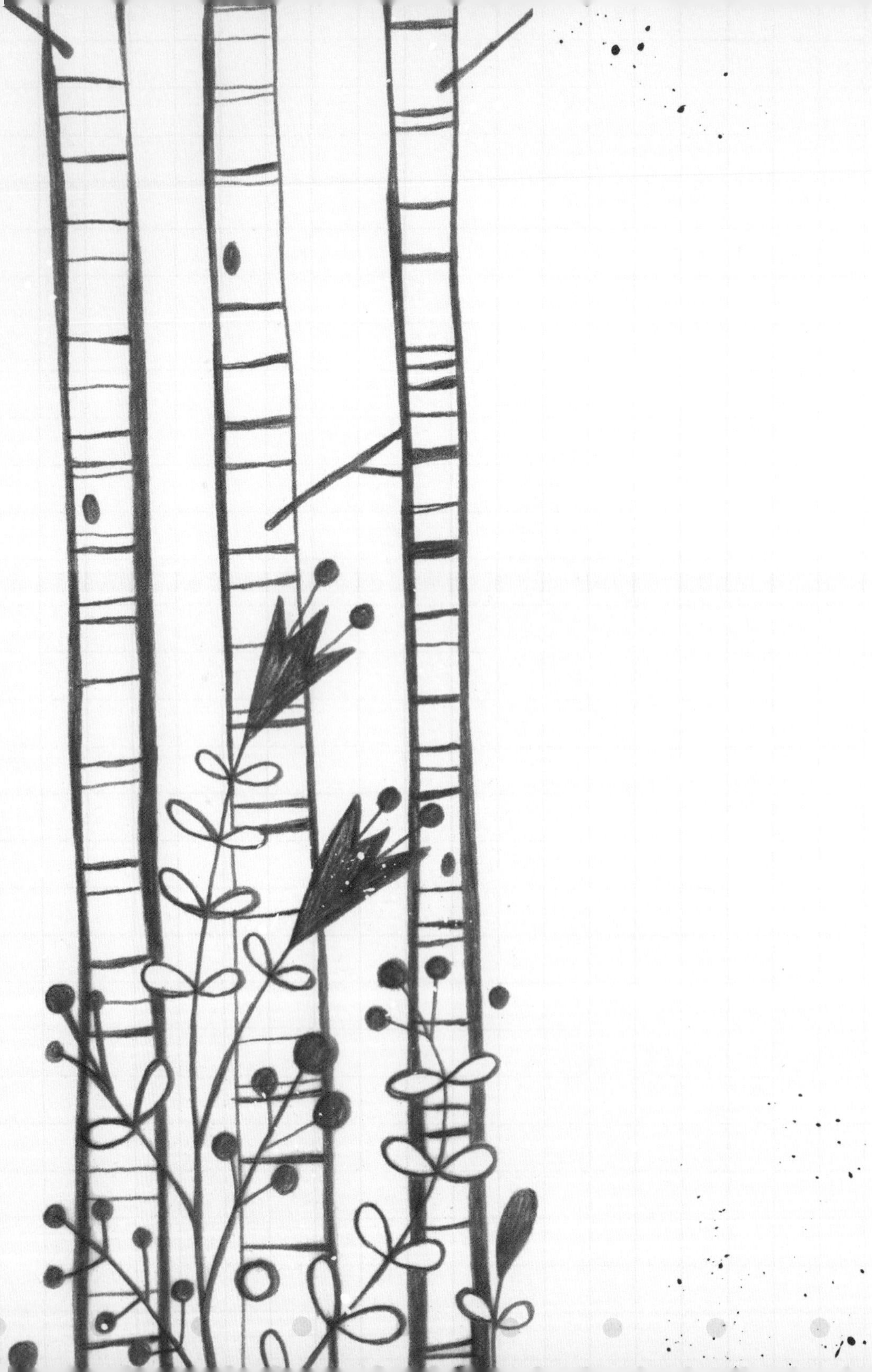

GOLDILOCKS CLEARLY
DIDN'T KNOW WHO
SHE WAS DEALING WITH.

MOMENT-KEEPER
DAY-MAKER
LIFE-CHANGER

It's a Mama Bear thing.

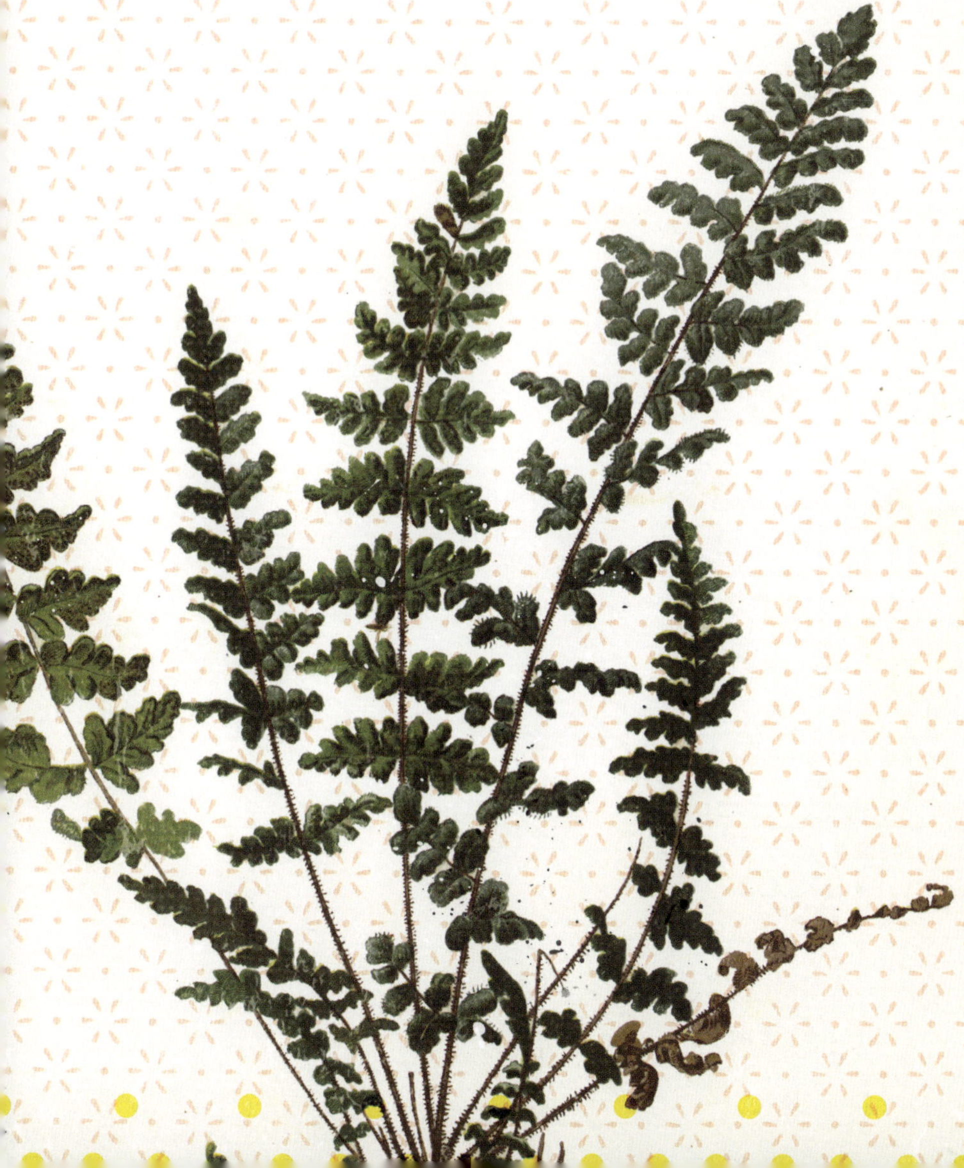

SHE'S A LOVER, NOT A FIGHTER, BUT YOU BETTER BELIEVE SHE'LL FIGHT FOR THE ONES SHE LOVES.

SIGN #49
YOU'RE A MAMA BEAR

Your hugs are just this side of "too tight."

HOW TO RESPOND WHEN

MAMA BEAR

TALKS:

1. Listen up.

2. Listen good.

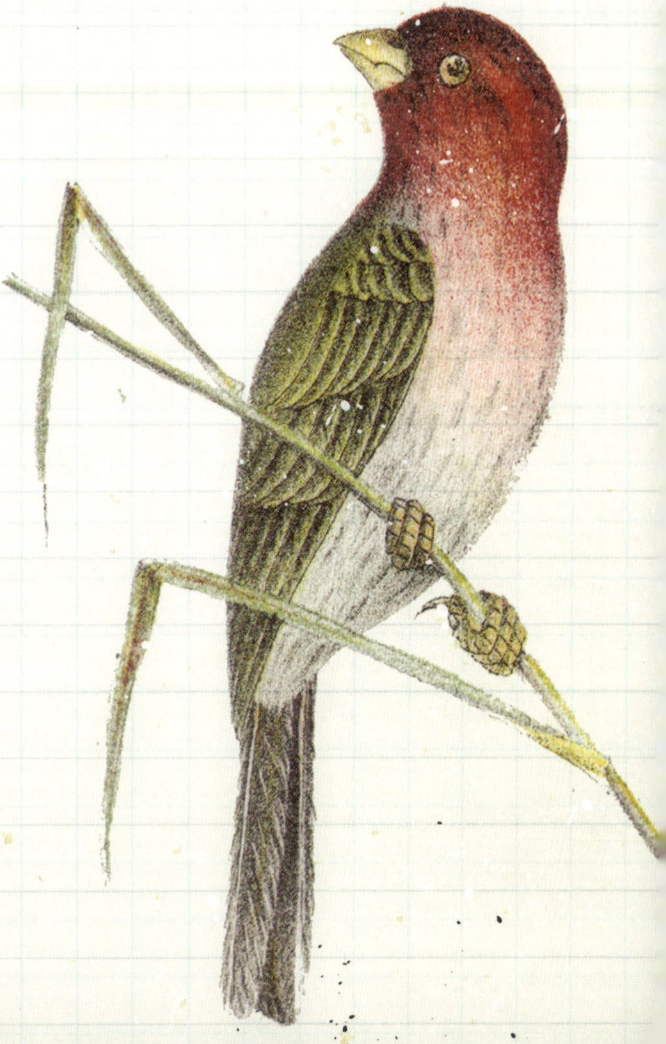

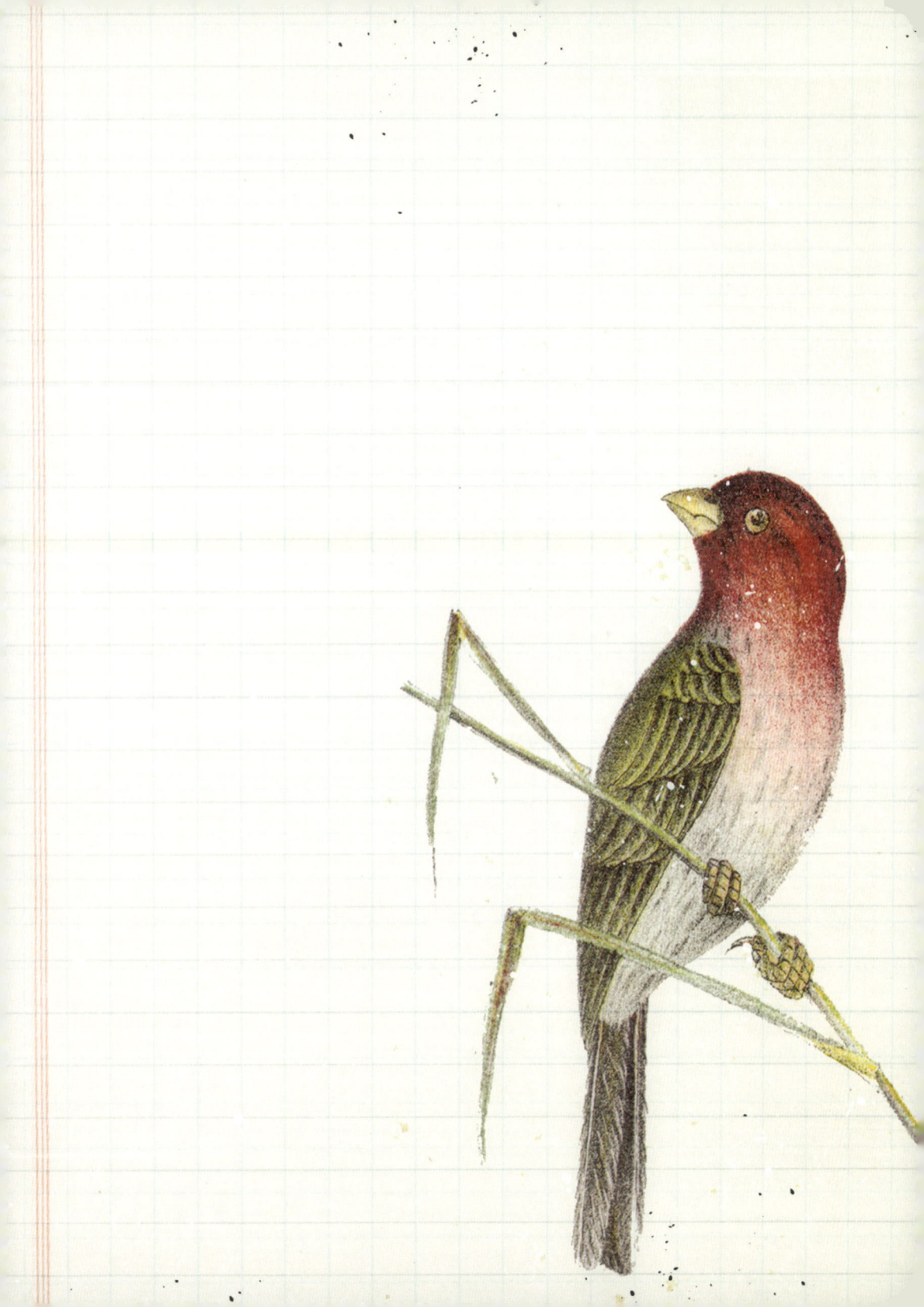

Mama Bear

OCCASIONALLY SHARP CLAWS.
ALWAYS SOFT HEART.

WHEN SHE HUGS YOU,
YOU STAY HUGGED.

(BUT SHE'LL ALWAYS HUG
YOU AGAIN JUST IN CASE.)

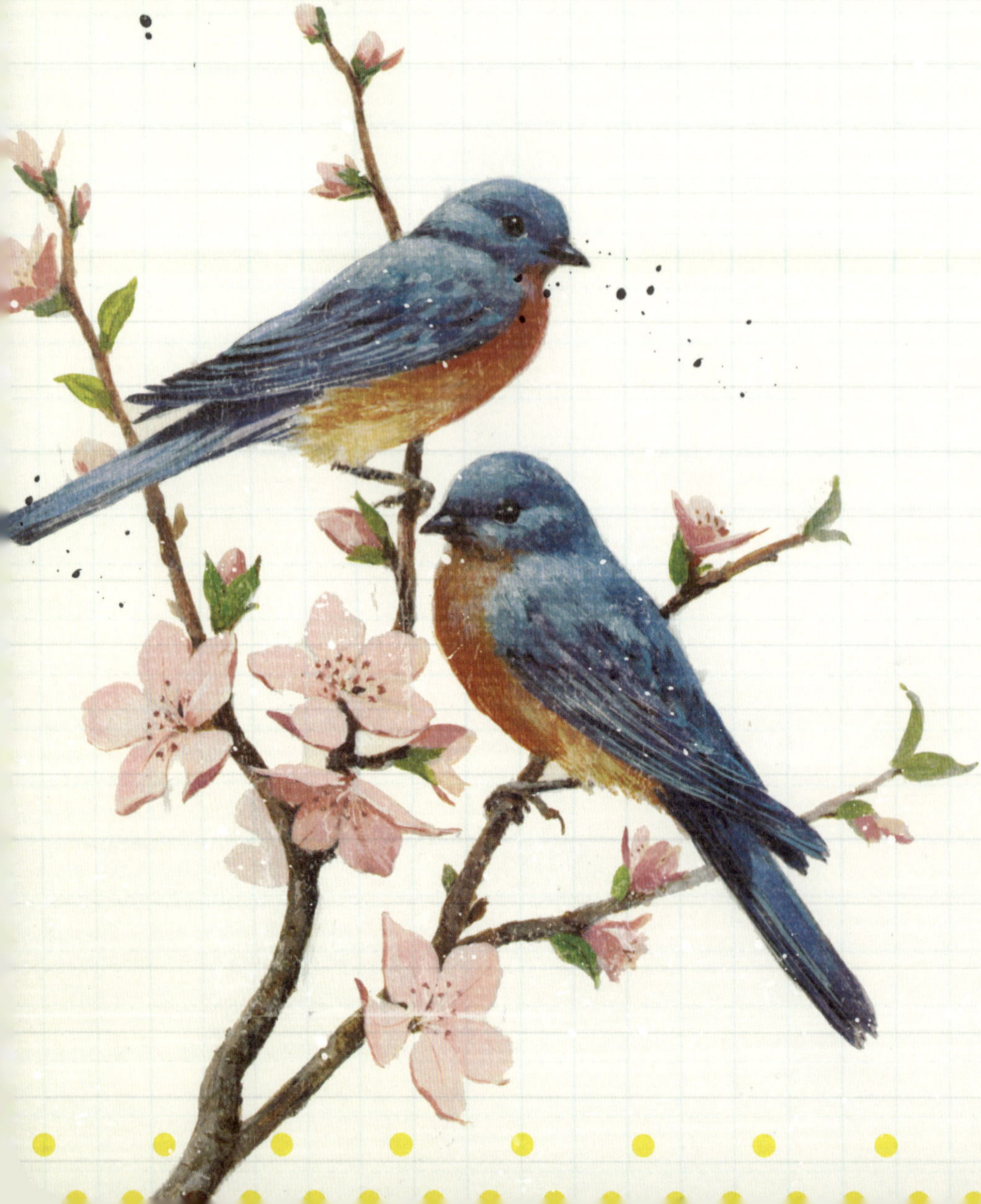

WHY DID THE MAMA BEAR CROSS THE ROAD?

Love.

SAME REASON FOR EVERYTHING SHE DOES.

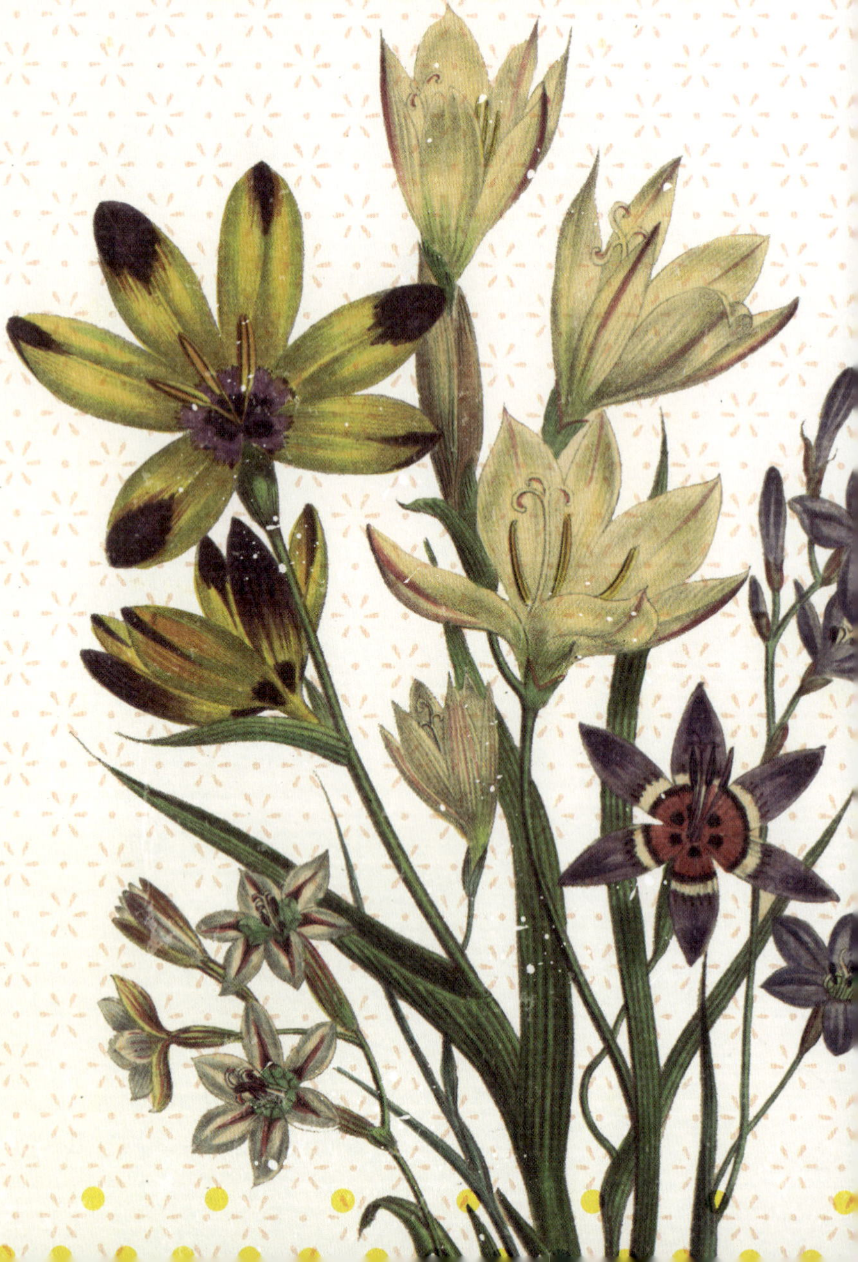

HER HEART IS...
BEAUTIFULLY FIERCE
FIERCELY BEAUTIFUL

SHE IS A RARE BREED...

EQUAL PARTS HUGGER,
HELPER, FEELER,
AND FIGHTER.

SIGN #56
YOU'RE A MAMA BEAR

You're equal parts "Go get 'em, Kid!" and "Come to Mama, Sweetie."

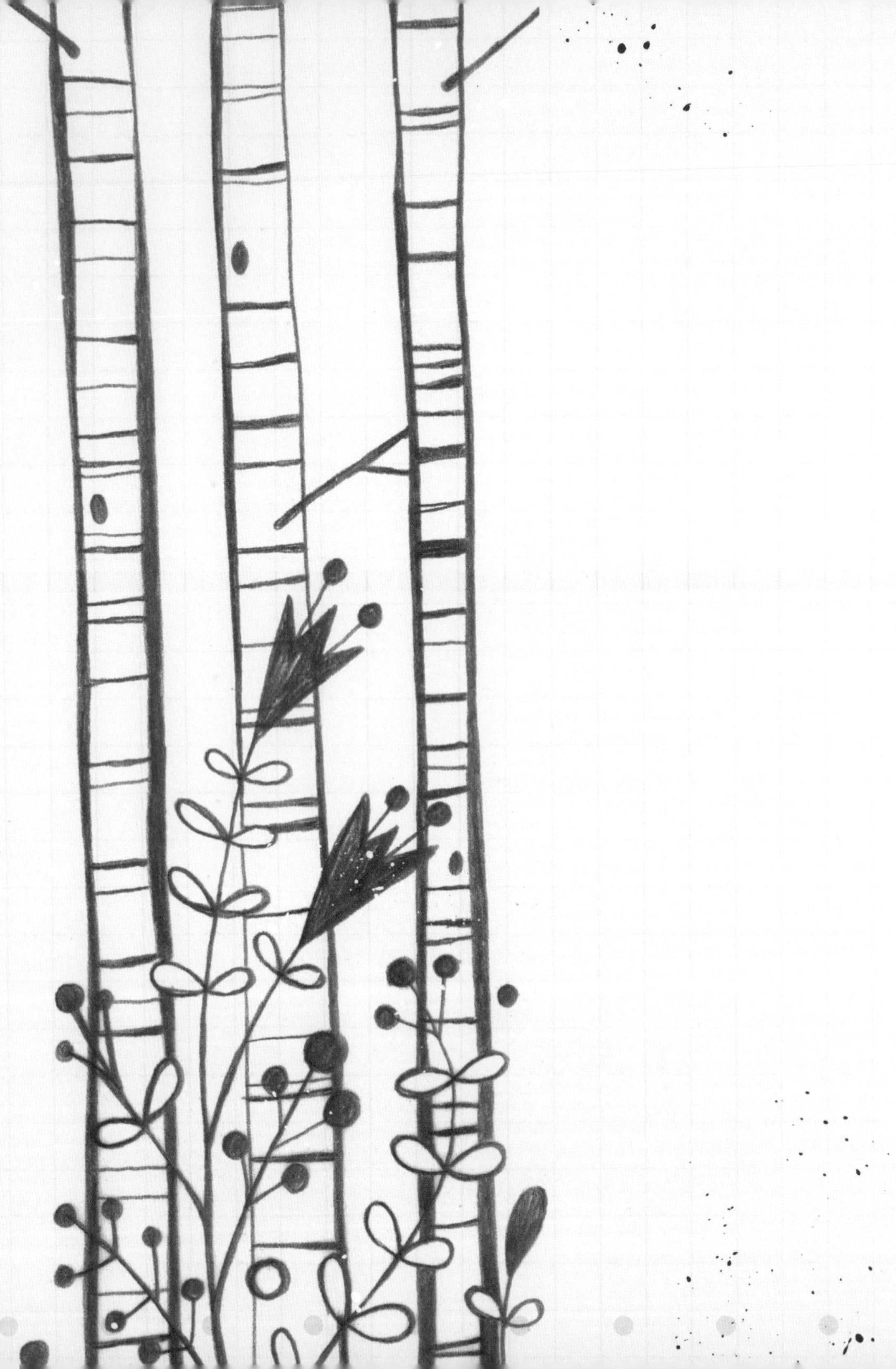

HOW TO CALM AN ANGRY MAMA BEAR:

1. Check to see if you have come between her and her cub.

2. If so, MOVE.

3. Back away slowly, keeping both hands visible.

4. Murmur sincere and soothing apologetic words.

5. Follow any instructions she gives <u>exactly</u>.

IGNORE THE FAINT HUMMING SOUND COMING FROM HER GENERAL DIRECTION.

That's just her major protective vibe.

"SHE'S A BIT OF A PUSHOVER,"
SAID NO ONE EVER.

SHE IS MAMA BEAR, HEAR HER ROAR.

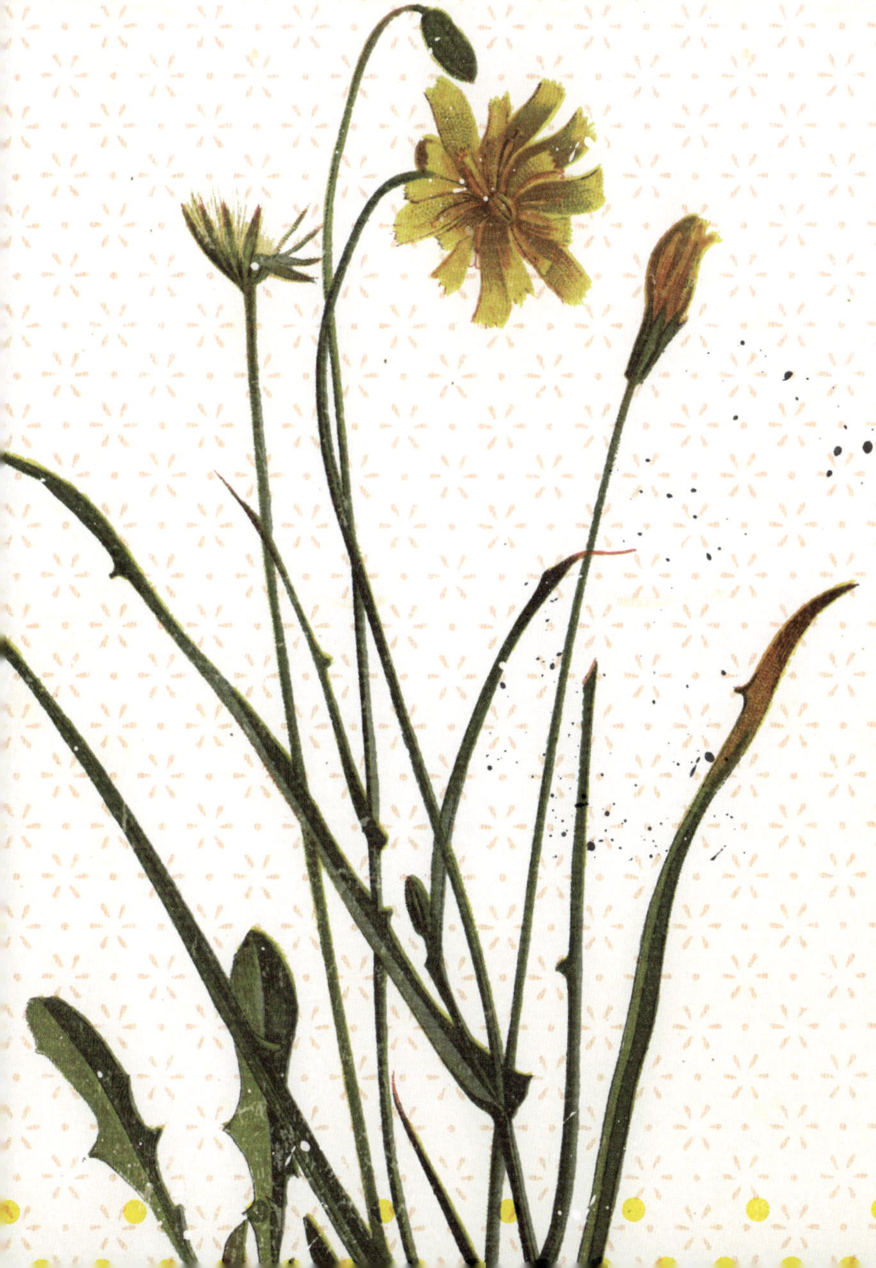

Mama Bear Math

THE SHORTEST DISTANCE BETWEEN HER AND HER CHILD IS A STRAIGHT LINE RIGHT THROUGH ANYONE FOOLISH ENOUGH TO BE STANDING IN THE WAY.

SHE CAN CONVEY
"don't even think about it"
WITH JUST ONE LOOK.

STANDING UP.
SPEAKING UP.
LIFTING UP...
IT'S A MAMA
BEAR THING.

SIGN #65
YOU'RE A MAMA BEAR

You love your family with all your heart, soul, and strength.

They love you that way, too.

WHAT MAMA BEAR SAYS

"DON'T FORGET YOUR JACKET."

"EAT YOUR VEGGIES."

"BECAUSE I SAID SO."

"DON'T MAKE ME TELL YOU AGAIN."

"JUST WAIT UNTIL YOU HAVE KIDS."

WHAT SHE MEANS

———— I LOVE YOU.

———— I LOVE YOU.

——— BECAUSE SHE SAID SO.

—— DON'T MAKE HER TELL YOU AGAIN. SERIOUSLY.

— THEN, YOU'LL UNDERSTAND HOW MUCH I LOVE YOU.

SHE IS UNBEATABLY STRONG, UNENDINGLY LOYAL, UNSTOPPABLY LOVING.

HER LOVE PICKS YOU UP, SETS YOU STRAIGHT, *and gives you an oh-so-gentle shove in the right direction.*

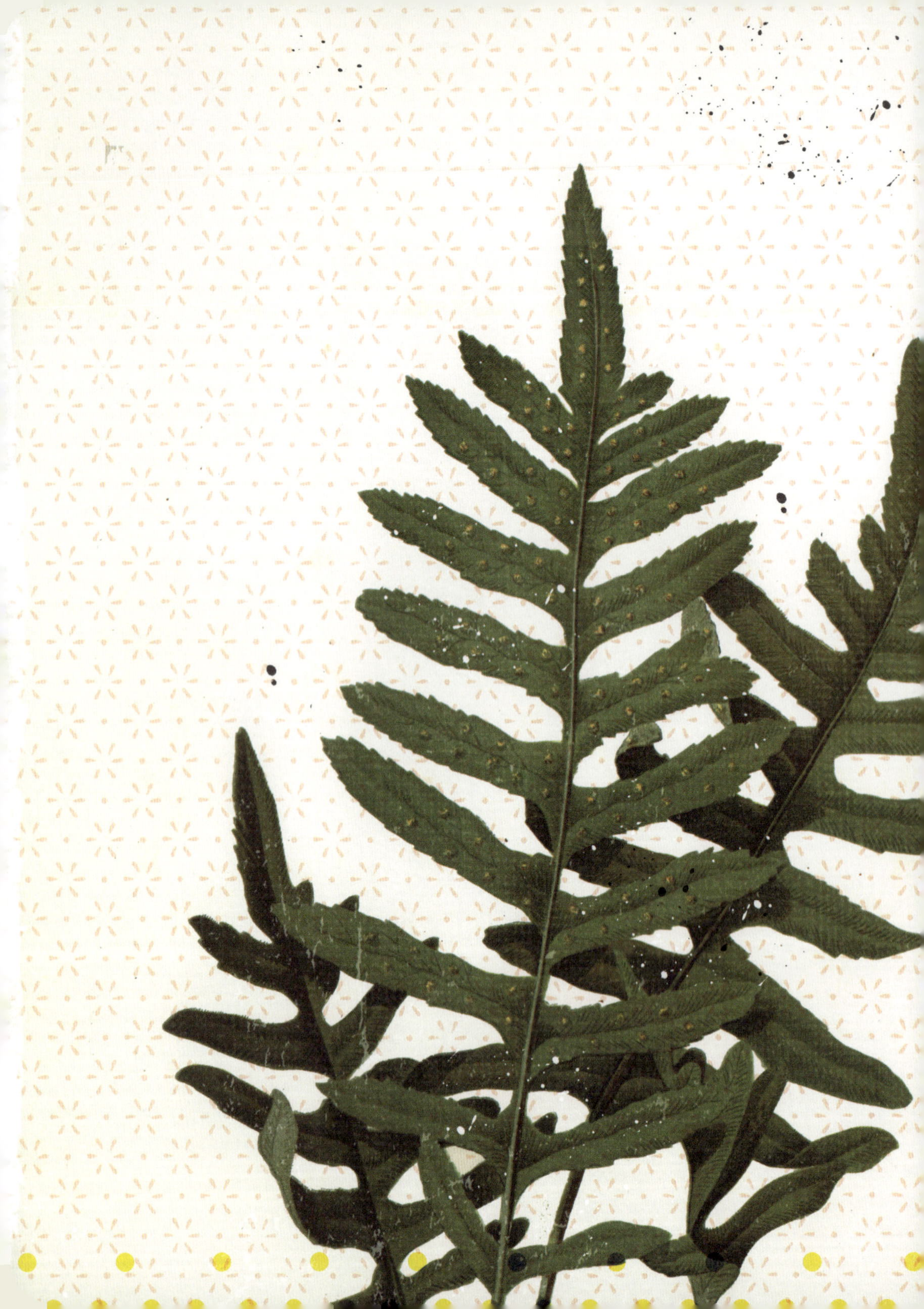

CIA GOT NOTHIN' ON MAMA BEARS.

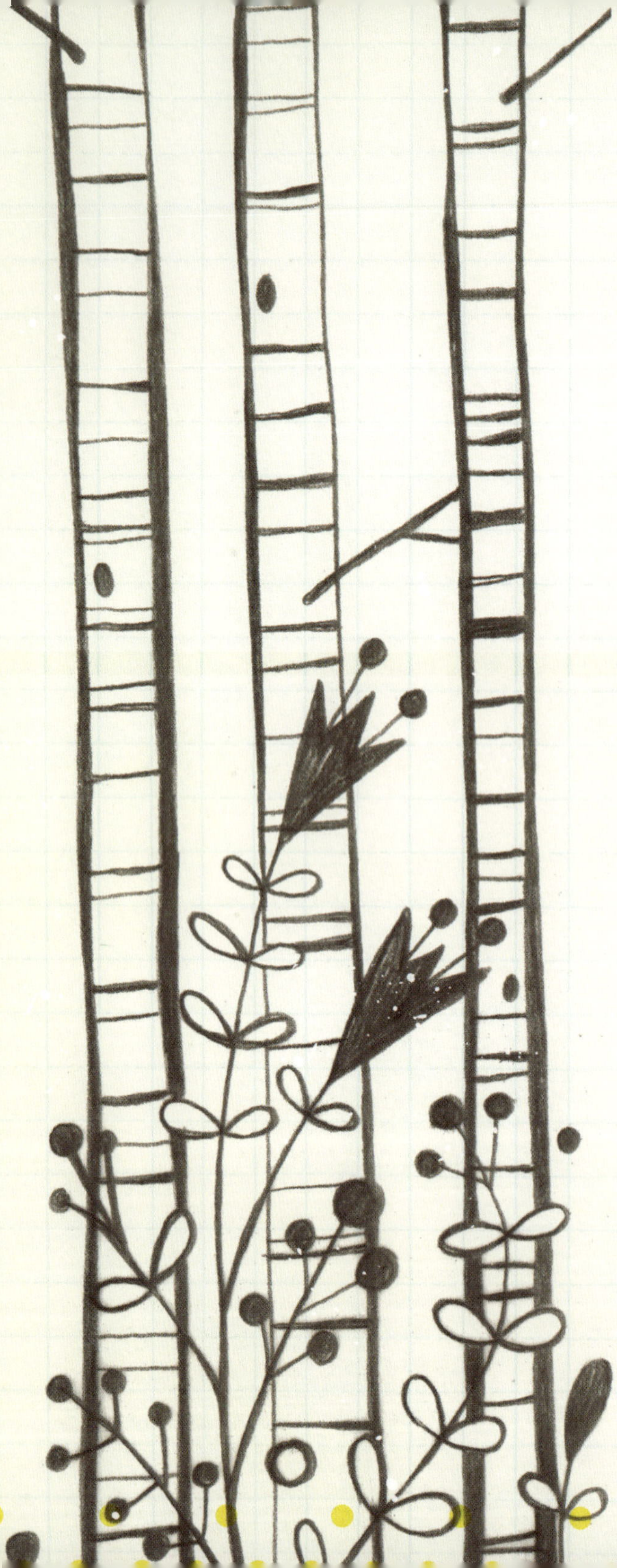

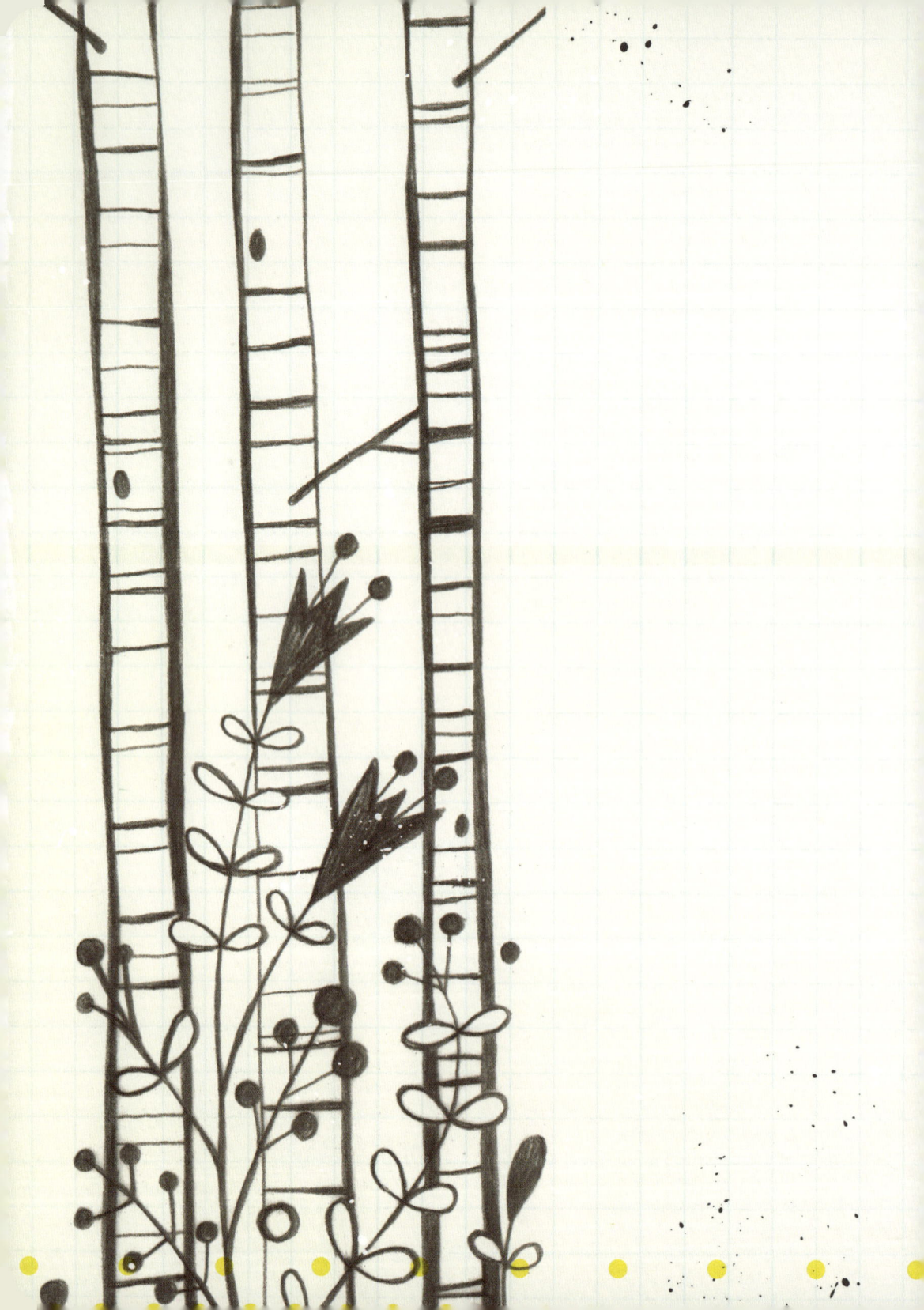

HOW TO HUG LIKE A
MAMA BEAR:

1. Wrap your whole self around hug recipient.

2. Hold on.

3. Hold on.

4. Never be the first to let go.

NOTE:
IF YOU CAN DO SOMETHING ELSE WHILE GIVING THE HUG, YOU'RE DOING IT WRONG.

IN HER CAR, EVERYONE MUST BUCKLE UP EVERY SINGLE TIME....

But she's still been known to shoot out a "mom seatbelt arm" for good measure.

DRIVEN
BY INSTINCT,
FUELED BY
LOVE....IT'S
A MAMA BEAR
THING.

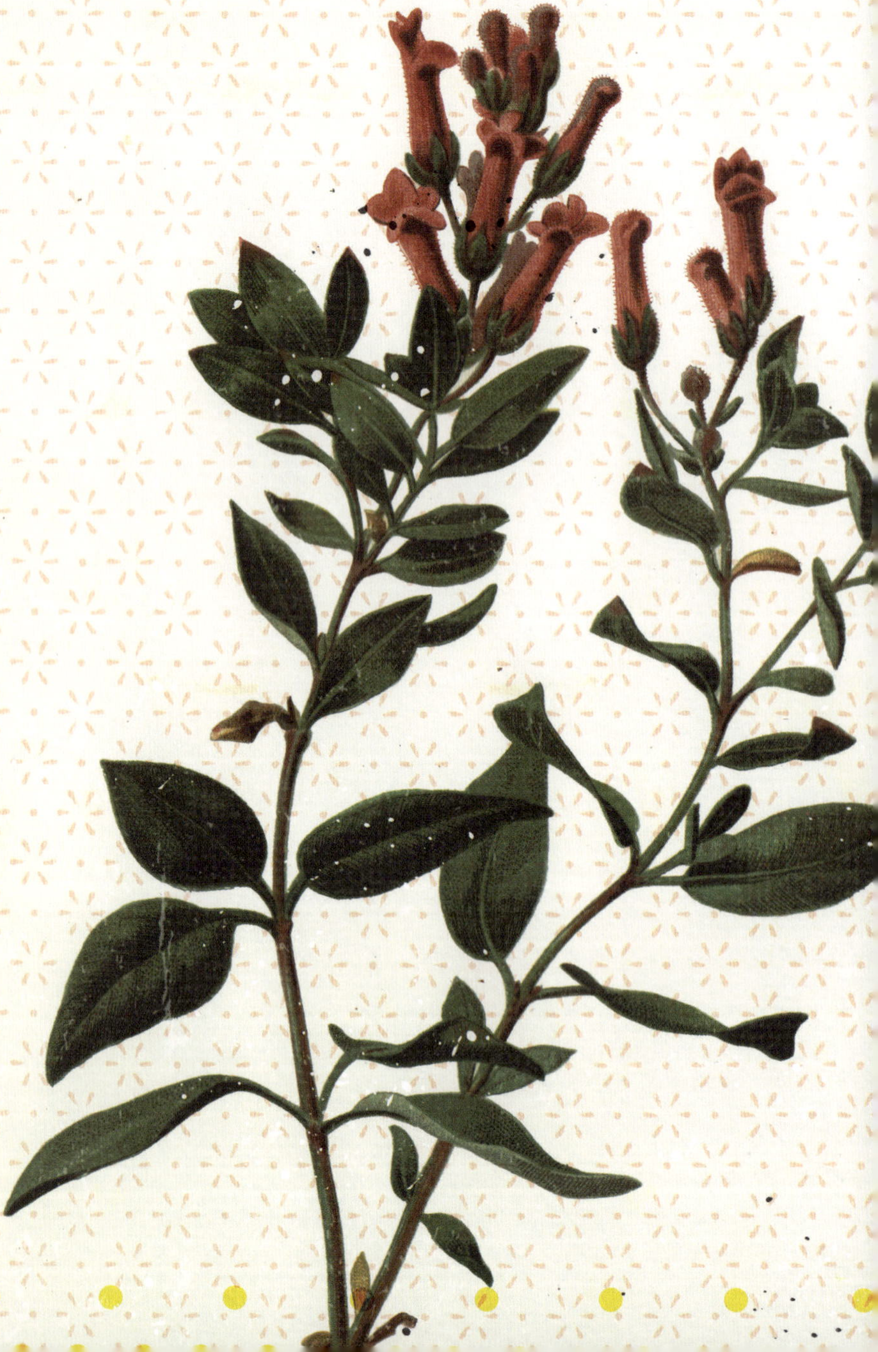

SHE MAKES EVERYONE SHE LOVES FEEL LIKE SHE LOVES THEM BEST.

SHE DOESN'T ALWAYS MOVE MOUNTAINS FOR THE ONES SHE LOVES.

BUT WHEN SHE DOES, STEP WAY BACK AND WATCH FOR AVALANCHES.

SIGN #72
YOU'RE A MAMA BEAR

You're intense when necessary, tough when tested, and loving always.

WHEN SHE TELLS YOU SHE LOVES YOU, YOU STAY TOLD.

(But of course, she's happy to tell you again anytime.)

WHEN A MAMA BEAR WILL GIVE UP ON YOU:

1. Never

2. At no time

3. Not once

4. All of the above

EMBRACING THE LOVE AND CHAOS OF MOTHERHOOD WITH ARMS OPEN WIDE....

It's a Mama Bear thing.

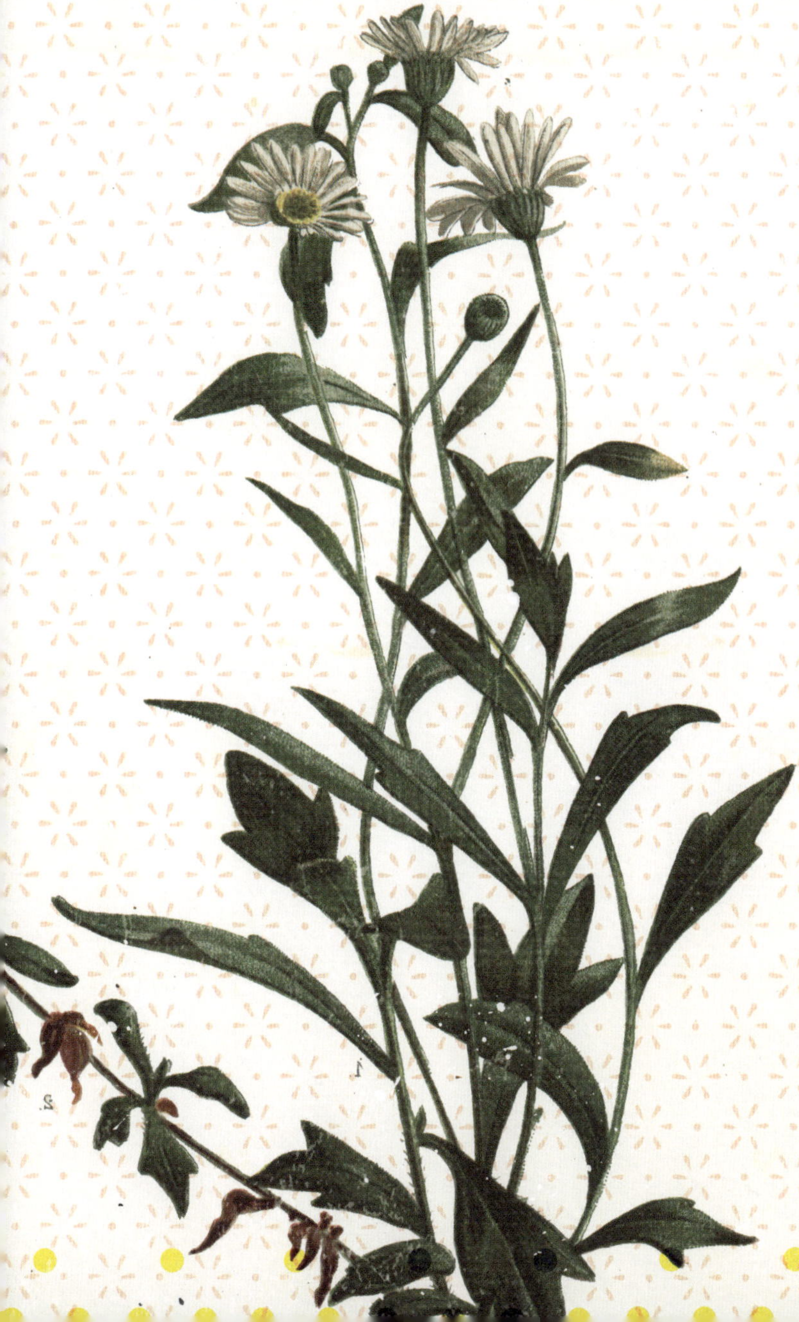

SHE WON'T BACK DOWN. SHE WILL NOT GIVE IN.

Where her kids are concerned,

SHE'S IN IT TO WIN.

SIGN #89
YOU'RE A MAMA BEAR

You've contemplated throwing down with someone who's hurt your child's feelings. You didn't, of course, but . . .

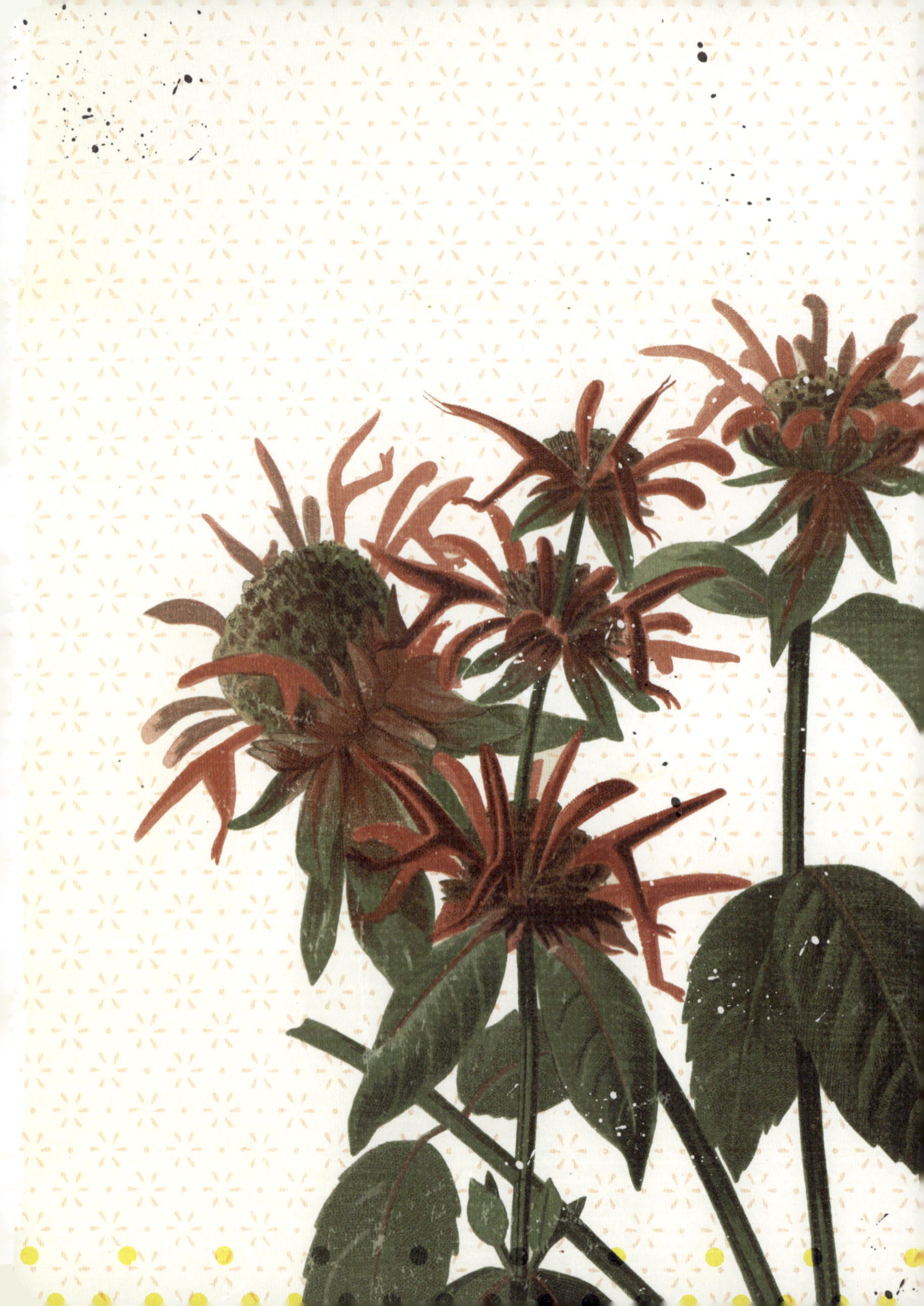

**SHE DOES RIGHT.
SHE DOES TOUGH.
SHE DOES WARM AND KIND.
SHE DOES GOOD.
REALLY GOOD.**

She's Mama Bear, and no one else does it all quite like her.

FORGET THE DOG.

BEWARE THE MOM.

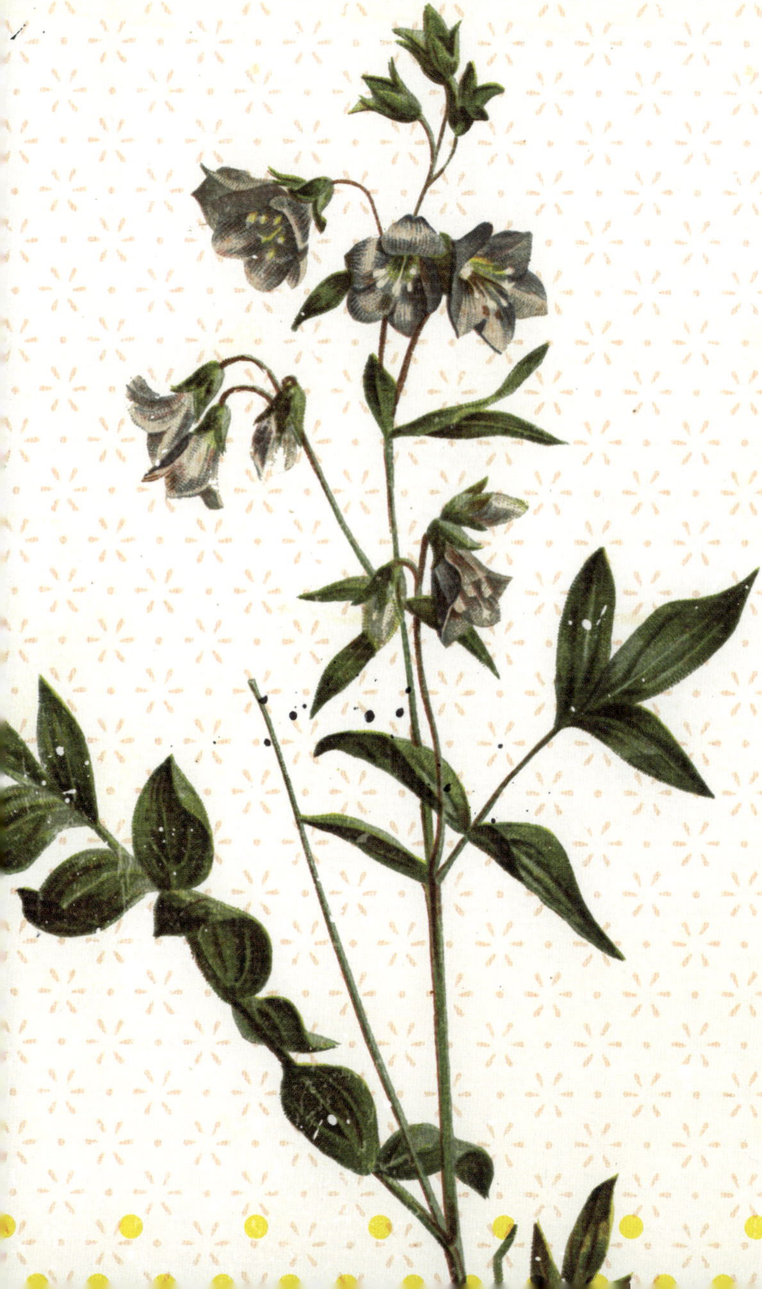

SIGN #91
YOU'RE A MAMA BEAR

You've never actually had to growl at anyone, but if the need arises, you're totally ready.

SHE'S A SPECIAL FORCE OF NATURE...

ALWAYS LIFE-GIVING AND ONLY OCCASIONALLY TERRIFYING.

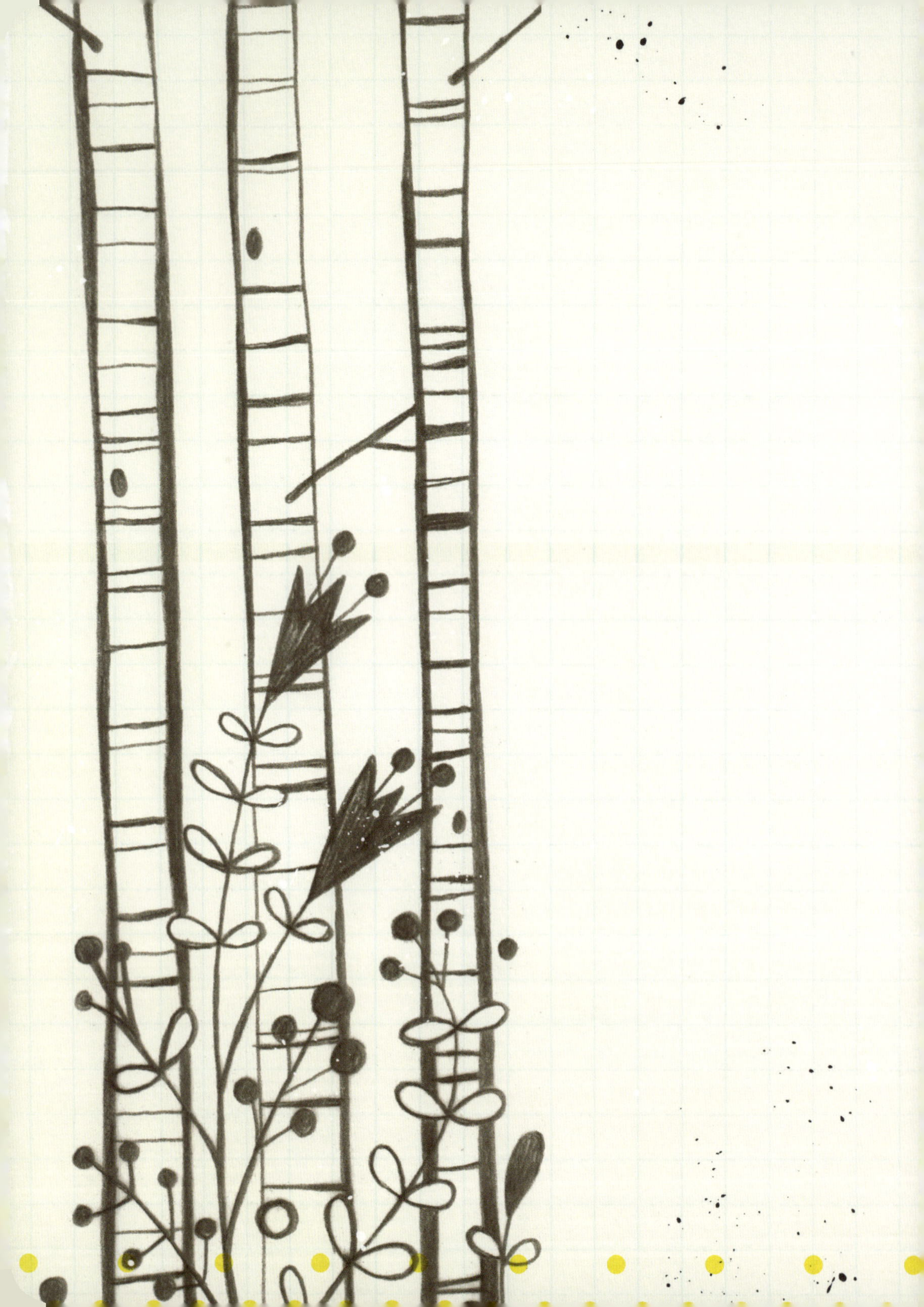

SHE MAY NOT BE
COMPLETELY FEARLESS.
BUT SHE'S NEVER LET
IT SLOW HER DOWN YET.

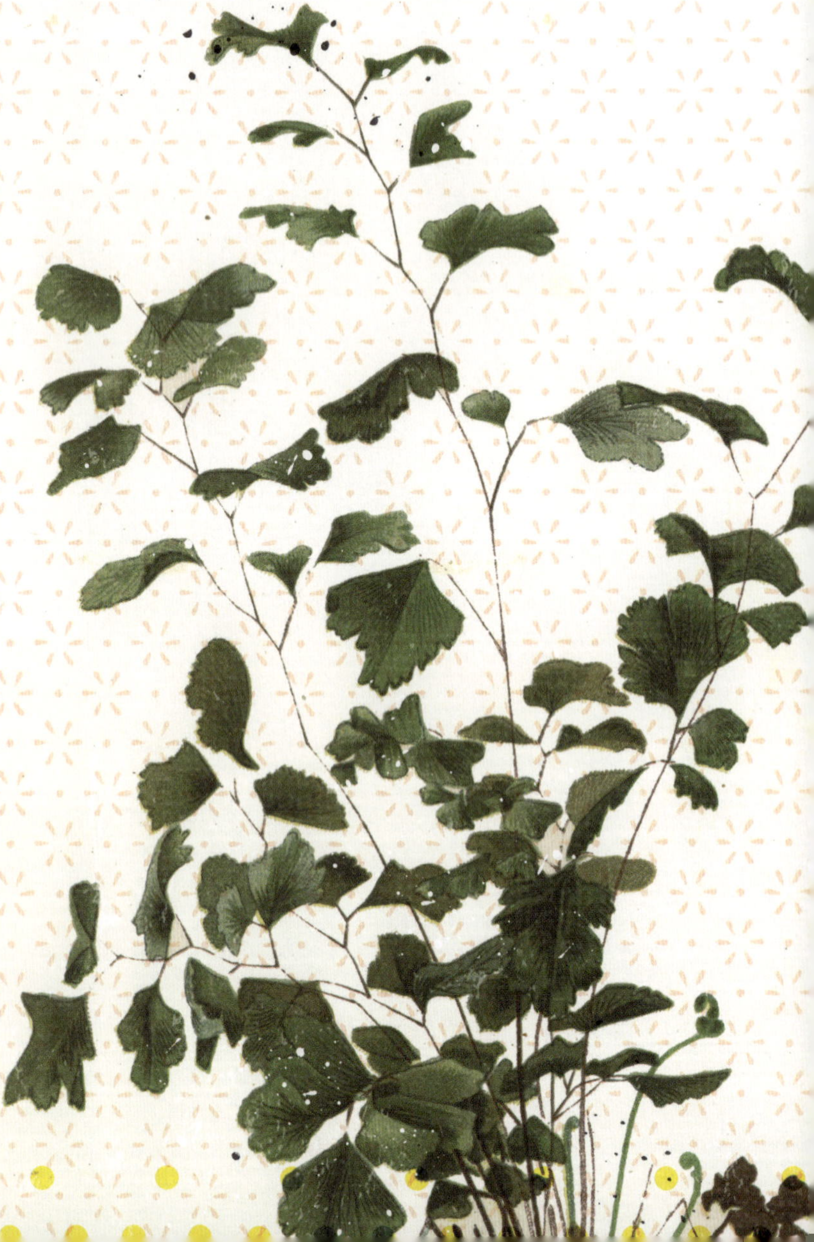

**DANGEROUS TO CROSS.
HARD TO SHOCK.
EASY TO LOVE . . .**

It's a Mama Bear thing.

HOW TO THANK A
MAMA BEAR:

1. With hugs

2. With to-do's checked off her list

3. With more hugs

4. With snacks

5. With "I love yous"

SIGN #106
YOU'RE A MAMA BEAR

You've discovered fears you never knew existed but also strengths you never knew you had.

SHE'S GOT HER FAMILY'S BACK FOREVER AND EVER AND EVER . . .

If you enjoyed this book
or it has touched your life in some way,
we'd love to hear from you.

Please write a review at Hallmark.com,
e-mail us at booknotes@hallmark.com,
or send your comments to:

Hallmark Book Feedback
P.O. Box 419034
Mail Drop 100
Kansas City, MO 64141